V.M. Rabolú

HERCOLUBUS

OR RED PLANET

HERCOLUBUS
OR RED PLANET

HERCOLUBUS OR RED PLANET
Joaquín Enrique Amórtegui Valbuena
(V. M. Rabolú)

Title of the Colombian Original Issue:
HERCÓLUBUS O PLANETA ROJO

The presentation of this work is the property of the author.

Copyright © C. Volkenborn Verlag
Postfach 11 16
63611 Bad Orb, Germany.

ISBN 978-3-934192-48-5

Printed by: Litoprint- Artes Gráficas. Lda.
                         Vale do grou Portugal

CONTENTS

CONTENTS

PREFACE

I have written this book with great sacrifice, lying in bed unable to stand or to sit up. But seeing the need to warn Humanity of the coming catastrophe, I made a great effort.

I dedicate this message to this Humanity, as a last resort, because there is nothing else to do.

(V. M. Rabolú)

HERCOLUBUS
OR RED PLANET

Humanity is captivated by the predictions of those we wrongly call scientists, who do nothing but fill Humanity with lies and distort the truth. We are going to talk about Hercolubus or Red Planet, which is approaching Earth.

According to the scientists they have weighed it, and they say it is so many tons and has certain diameter as if it were a child's toy, but this is not the case. Hercolubus or Red Planet is five or six times larger than Jupiter. It is a gigantic mass, which can not be stopped or deflected.

The Earth's inhabitants believe that it is a toy, but in fact it is the beginning of the end for the planet Earth. It has already arrived. The other worlds of our solar system know this and they are making every effort to help us avoid this catastrophe. However, nobody will be able to stop it. This is the punishment we deserve to put an end to so much wickedness.

I state that Hercolubus is a creation like our world. It is inhabited by its own Humanity, which is also perverse like our own. Each planet, each world has its own Humanity. Scientists should not believe that they can attack and disintegrate Hercolubus. Its inhabitants also have weapons, which would respond and eliminate us instantly. If they are attacked, they will defend themselves and the end will come faster.

Within the to-and-fro movement of life, everything returns to its beginning or to its end. The same thing happened with less intensity on the continent of Atlantis. However, in this return of events, our planet will not be able to bear the other planet passing very close without breaking into pieces. This is what the scientists ignore, they believe that they are very powerful and that their weapons are capable of destroying this giant planet. They are very mistaken.

In a short time, the destruction of the famous "Tower of Babel" that they have built will take place. They have already finished it and negative consequences are now coming for the whole of Humanity

The scientists can deny this with their theories, as they are doing now and have done before: they distort the truth because of pride, conceit and ambition for power. They will laugh like braying donkeys, because they are not able to measure the consequences of what they have done. They have placed nuclear bombs all over the planet in order to control it, without considering that God and his Justice exists, and will crush everything. You can not talk to beasts about God because they bray and deny him through their actions. They believe they are gods, and they are not.

The false, so-called powers that exist today will become ruined economically as well as morally. Money will disappear within a very short time. Hunger and misery will put an end to them. They will not be able to endure a single violent shake, and they will remain paralyzed by fear and terror. Then they will truly realize that the Divine Justice exists to punish evil.

At present, the whole world is distracted looking for money at any cost. This is precisely what happened in Atlantis where the god of that epoch was money: religions represented it as a golden calf.

In the same way in this epoch, money is the god. This is totally wrong.

The rich, who now brag so much of power, will be the most unfortunate. Having a lot of money will gain them nothing when there is no one to sell to them and no one who buys from them. They will kneel and weep when begging for a plate of food, and they will howl like dogs.

When Hercolubus comes closer to the Earth and is set next to the Sun, deadly epidemics will begin to spread over the entire planet. Neither doctors nor official science will know what sort of illnesses they are or how to cure them. They will be powerless in the face of the epidemics. Life will begin to disappear from our planet. At that point, Humanity will have to eat its own corpses because of overwhelming hunger and unbearable heat.

The moment of tragedy and darkness will come: tremors, earthquakes and tidal waves. Human beings will become mentally unbalanced, because they will not be able to eat or sleep. In the face of danger, they will throw themselves into the abyss in masses, completely mad.

This race will disappear. No life will be left on the planet and the Earth will sink into the ocean. This is because Humanity has reached the highest level of depravity. It already wants to pass on the evil to other planets but this will not be allowed.

Scientists and the whole world are full of panic even before the destruction has started. However, the fear of God does not exist in any inhabitant of the Earth. They believe that they are lords and masters of life and that they are powerful, but now they are going to see that certainly there is Divine Justice which judges us according to our deeds.

What I affirm in this book is a prophecy that will be fulfilled very shortly, because I have evidence about the end of the planet: I know it. I am not scaring but warning, because I am distressed about this poor Humanity. These events will not wait and there is no time to waste with illusory things.

NUCLEAR TESTS
AND THE OCEAN

We are in a blind alley.

We have already spoken about Hercolubus in a rather superficial way, without going into much detail, so as not to scare or alarm people. We are going to see another fatal and destructive danger, which no one will be able to stop: the nuclear tests in the ocean.

There are large, very deep cracks along the seabed, which are already reaching the fire within the Earth. This is happening precisely because of nuclear tests that the scientists and powers - they believe themselves to be powers - are carrying out. They do not measure the consequences of the barbarity they have committed and continue committing against the planet and against Humanity.

The fire within the Earth has already started to make contact with the water, and cyclones have started to appear. North Americans call it "The Niño Phenomenon". It is not "El Niño", it is the contact between the fire within the Earth and the water, and this is spreading in the ocean. As cracking develops, tidal waves, earthquakes and frightening occurrences in water and on land will take place. There will be no coastal town that will not be devastated. The planet will begin sinking into the ocean since the Earth's axis has already been shifted. This is because of all the tests that are being carried out.

The Earth's axis is already shifted from its position, and through tremors, earthquakes and tidal waves, it will become completely loose and sinking will take place. Do not believe, dear reader, that the planet will sink suddenly. This is a long, slow, distressing and painful process, through which Humanity will have to go. It will sink piece by piece into the ocean until it reaches its end.

Scientists do not measure the atrocities they have committed against Creation. They will be victims of their own inventions. There are already monsters or wild beasts on the seabed, which have fed on nuclear energy. The increase in temperature of the water will make them come out and look for refuge. They will reach the coastal towns and will devastate everything: houses, buildings, ships and people. These wild beasts which have developed from nuclear energy are nuclear, and because of this, three-dimensional bullets will do nothing but make them more furious. What I am saying here will happen in a short time.

And this does not stop here. The boiling of the seawater caused by the fire of the Earth will cause an immense steam to rise: neither planes will be able to fly nor ships navigate. This steam will cloud the sun, total darkness will come and life on our planet will come to an end. I advise you, dear reader, not to leave from where you are, because there is nowhere you can go.

Scientists ignore all these consequences that they have provoked with their nuclear explosions and their tests in the ocean. So then, no matter how scientific they are, they are ignorant, wild beasts who do not care about inventing devices to destroy Humanity and themselves.

Nuclear energy contaminated the whole sea and the animals living in it. It stands to reason that when we eat fish or certain seafood we are contaminating ourselves. As a recommendation, it is better not to eat it.

The sea inhales and exhales because it is a living body. When exhaling, it contaminates the oxygen that we breathe and all the vegetation. Changes in the human organism will occur and monstrous children will be born caused by this general contamination, alarming the whole world.

When looking at our planet from other superior dimensions, you can see it has already disappeared. What we see is a yellow colored mudhole, as if you were boiling a bit of soil with water in a pot. You see no life at all of any species, plant, animal or human. Everything is dead. All that is needed is for this to crystallize in the Third Dimension or the physical world so that it begins to vanish from the face of the Earth, as everything comes from above to below.

The scientists and the intellectuals will laugh at the top of their voices like braying donkeys at what I am saying here, but when the moment comes, they will be the most cowardly. They will cry without knowing what they should do or where they should go.

Well, what do we expect from Humanity? We expect its end. Those who falsely call themselves scientists are certainly scientists, but destructive, not constructive. They are using science to destroy everything that has life.

I am asking the scientists, the ones who are braying so loud: what formula can you find to evade these problems that are threatening to destroy Humanity and this planet? There is no formula other than to await the catastrophe. Or, if you have an effective formula could you inform us about it?

EXTRATERRESTRIALS

I have seen films and magazines by North Americans, trying to block out the light of the sun with one finger, but they are mistaken. They will not blur my vision and will certainly not make me believe in their stupid theories and vile imaginations, as they are doing with Humanity.

Just as they are doing with Hercolubus, which is rapidly approaching Earth, by putting it down (daring to state its weight and mass) so they have done with extraterrestrials by distorting them as gorillas, as animals. This is a big lie, one hundred percent false, because the inhabitants of the other planets of our solar system and our galaxy are superior humans and wise beings.

I have had contact with extraterrestrials many times. I have been on Venus and on Mars by consciously travelling in my Astral Body and I can certify and testify to these marvelous inhabitants. I can not find words to describe their wisdom, their culture and the angelic life that they live.

Life on Venus

The Venusians have perfect bodies: a wide or broad forehead, blue eyes, straight nose, blond hair and an astonishing intelligence. They are more or less between 1.3 and 1.4 meters (4'3"-4'6" feet) tall. Nobody is taller or shorter. There are no potbellies and you do not see deformed people. Everybody has an angelic figure: there is perfection in men and women because it is a planet with an ascendant, superior Humanity. There are no monsters like those you can see here.

They wear a wide belt full of red, blue and yellow buttons all around, which flash like a lighthouse. When in danger, they press a main button, which you can imagine is like a buckle we have on our belt. Just by pressing it, a circle of fire is formed which can destroy a bullet and everything that it catches around it.

I also found out about a pocket manual weapon, the size of a cigarette pack. Just by pressing a button on the gadget, they could blow up a hill, however big it might be, and make it disappear. What would an inhabitant of the Earth do with a weapon like this?

When you think of asking them a question, without you needing to move your lips, they give you the answer in whichever language it may be, as they speak all languages perfectly. They have the Gift of Tongues.

When you are talking with a Venusian, the others carry on with their work and continue their business without stopping. They are not like us, who gather to look at and criticize a person with a physical defect. I have looked at myself on Venus and when comparing my figure with theirs, I felt ashamed: one appears like a gorilla. However, nobody is struck by that, everybody passes by without curiosity or surprise. It is an unheard of culture.

Now I am going to describe how their earth is, their nature, their way of living and how they work.

The earth on Venus is not compact or heavy like ours, but light and soft. As for stones, we might imagine them to be like those on our planet but this is not so. There are big, small,

all sorts of stones, but they do not have as much weight as they do here. They are not dense; you could lift a stone which would weigh pounds here, over there the weight is just ounces, nothing, because they are light and of a soft material.

The trees are not huge and the vegetation does not contain thorns and there are no vines in the mountains blocking the way. You can make your way through one of those mountains without needing to take a machete or a knife, because there is nothing to cut. There are not dangers anywhere.

The fruit trees are even sown on the flat roofs of houses in pots and with good fertilized soil, so that they bear fruit. There nobody takes a piece of fruit simply because they feel like doing so, but they wait until it is ripe and mellow. They harvest it with a device, without touching it with their hands, and it goes through tubes to tanks with very pure revolving water where it goes through a special cleaning process. After the fruit has been cleaned, it goes through another tube to machines where it is pulverized. From there it goes to another container where more vitamins are added, no chemical vitamins, but natural ones, and then it is sealed hermetically. This is one of their foods.

Regarding the sea, I believe that people will compare ours with theirs, but in fact their sea is perfectly blue, like a calm lagoon. There is no movement in any direction, no waves, that you can see into the deep without any artificial device.

Fish are extremely tame and are not afraid of anyone. There are areas in the sea where fish are fed with lots of vitamins. When it is necessary to eat some, they look to see which ones are the biggest or which ones they want to use. They carefully lay out a net there without damaging or frightening the other fish, then they take them out and gut them.

Then by means of some pulleys, the fish go into a tank with very pure revolving water, and they pass through a special cleaning process. This happens without touching them by hand. From there they go to machines, where the fish are pulverized. Further natural vitamins are added to the fish and this is another of their foods. The same is done with vegetables. Nobody eats meat of any kind there.

There are places, let us say like restaurants so that the reader understands better, where they go and sit at a table. Because there all the inhabitants read thoughts, it is not necessary to order the dish you would like to have. The dish arrives without you moving your lips. Expressing thanks and such things are not done as we do here. Once you have eaten, you stand up from the table and you do not have to ask how much it costs, how much you have to pay, or to say thanks, because everyone expresses thanks with a movement of the head.

The same thing happens with the clothes shops. When they want to change, they go into a shop and immediately they receive clothes and shoes. Right there they can press a button on the wall and a dark room is formed, where they can change and wash if they like. By pressing another button a jet of water flows out. Afterwards they hand over the clothing that they have just removed, so that it undergoes a special cleaning process. There are no differences in clothes or shoes: they are uniform for everybody.

Nobody owns a house there: when a Venusian couple is tired or would like to rest, a button is pressed in a house or a building, forming a dark room. When another button is pressed, a bed appears. Without needing to say "that belongs to me", whoever needs it uses it, without asking anybody for permission.

The streets on Venus are not like ours, the avenues move like an escalator. There are no accidents of any kind because everything is in order. The vehicles are very beautiful, richly decorated platforms. They depart, reach their destination and the platform descends with all the people on it. It is not the people who get down but the platform. Then, another platform goes up, which is already with other people, in order to continue its journey. These streets move with solar energy, every machine works with solar energy. Neither oil nor gasoline is used, or anything that causes pollution, for that reason pollution does not exist.

To build houses or buildings they do not go up as we do here, where you have to climb many meters to work. Everybody works from the ground. The roof of the building is the first thing they do, then they lift this level by means of some rollers and continue building the next floor. When it is ready, they lift it again with the rollers and so on, according to the number of floors that they want to build, without risking an accident.

Venusians, men and women, work two hours daily in their profession. Money does not exist there and nobody owns anything. Everybody has the right to everything and works for everyone. There is no Mr. so-and-so, because there exists equality. The law is to work two hours daily, so that there is neither hunger nor misery.

By using their powers and faculties they make nature work for them: they make it rain when they want, they make the Sun come out when they want or cloud over the sky. It is not as it is with us, where we are under the power of Nature.

There are no permits: "I need permission to travel to another planet", no. There, every Venusian can take a spaceship from the station in which they are kept, to travel where they wish, be it another planet or other galaxies, without asking anybody. There is total freedom with the commitment of leaving the spaceship where one found it when one returns, so that someone else can use it. There are no borders and no red tape.

I inform you that on Venus there are no families like on our planet, there are only couples. They have neither churches nor priests to get them married. They unite with their twin soul or their better half, as it is called who is the complement of every human being. There are no religions of any kind. The religion is the mutual respect towards life and others.

There exists no fornication like here, for the inhabitants of the Earth are worse than beasts. They use what Gnosis teaches: Scientific Chastity or Transmutation of the Energies. That is why they prolong their life as they want, because the energy is one's own life. By contrast on our planet, at an early age, people look old because of fornication.

When you shake hands with them, you feel an electrical current that shakes you as if you were receiving energy, because they are full of energy. They are not fornicators, as is the case here. They have such energy thanks to the Scientific Chastity.

They unite sexually to have children without fornication: one sperm that escapes is enough to create a physical body for a soul who wants to come to learn. There is no sexual degeneration as there is here, where priests are even marrying homosexuals. Homosexuality does not exist there: they are real men and real women. Sexual outrages are only seen on our planet, because on the other planets they know how to reproduce without falling into fornication.

When a child is born, he is transferred to a clinic with full care where he gets special food, until he is old enough to study. When he is old enough to begin preparation, he goes to a school, which is a huge workshop, where he will learn all the essentials in practice. In order to study the vocation that this soul carries within, the directors of those schools teach him how to use machinery and let him develop his own ideas.

When a child has an idea to produce something, the professors or teachers help the child to complete it until he makes the device he wants. They do so one by one with all of Humanity. Therefore, on Venus nobody is ignorant, everyone is prepared for the material and the spiritual ascent.

Life on Mars

Life on Mars is exactly the same as on Venus. There is freedom in everything. The Martians can move to any place on the planet, without needing papers or passports or anything like that, and without needing anyone's permission. Wherever they may go, there is a place to sleep, eat, clothing to change themselves, in whatever place on Mars. Wherever they may be, they find everything they need, because there are no borders but complete freedom. It is exactly the same way on the other planets of our solar system.

Martians have stronger bodies than Venusians, visibly more vigorous, for they belong to the Ray of Force.

On Mars everybody wears a soldier's uniform: shield, helmet and a suit of armor. All these war clothes are made of a material similar to bronze. They stand out because they are warriors to the core, but not warriors in the sense that we would call it here. There are no wars among them or with the other planets. Their war is directed against evil, to defeat evil, not against one another.

I inform you that on those planets nobody works using brutal force as we do in our world. Nobody sweats. They do not exhaust themselves because there the machines do the work. All of them are run by solar energy. What they do is to guide or operate the machines, where they relieve each other. Everything functions by the wisdom they have.

The extraterrestrials are so powerful that they are born, grow up and die at will. When they are tired of having a physical body for so many years and want to change, they die and are laid in a hollow exactly their size, which is in a wall. A door is closed and a button is pressed. They become ashes in a matter of minutes. If they were not quite dead, then the button does not work and they are taken out to die completely. There are no cemeteries. The ashes are scattered by a tree or buried. Nobody cries because of the death of a person: death for them is a change of clothes, nothing else.

In those worlds there is no involution in plants, animals, humanity or planets. Everything is ascending. By contrast, here we are descending with everything including the planet, as the facts prove. There are no plagues like flies, gnats or mosquitoes, which are harmful to health, or the threat of reptiles.

On Mars and on the other planets the law is to respect each other, life and everything. They respect the free will of each person. It is not as with the inhabitants of the Earth, who want to control the world purely by means of bullets and threats. The North Americans are very mistaken in the films and magazines that they release.

In this way I have described Mars a little to show the North Americans that they do not know anything about life on other worlds, as they deny the existence of life on Mars and other planets.

I do not use telescopes or anything artificial to know about the Universe. I know how to operate my inner bodies with complete will and consciousness. Gnosis passed on the keys to me. I put into practice what I was taught and the result was this: Knowing, for he who knows has Knowledge. He who does not have Knowledge talks of what he does not know. Gnosis in practice is beyond comparison: it overcomes all obstacles and barriers that may appear.

Interplanetary Spaceships

Let us talk a little about interplanetary spaceships. Scientists ignore them or call them into question, thus leading Humanity to doubt the existence of such ships.

All interplanetary spaceships move with solar energy. They are made from a material which does not exist here and which is resistant against bullets and everything. They are made of one piece, have no soldered joints or rivets, and are controlled by buttons.

They have two horizontal tubes made of a light material, very similar to aluminum but shinier and stronger, which does not exist on this planet. The tubes run through the spacecraft from the front to the rear. At the front solar energy enters and at the back the burned energy comes out. These are the fiery tails that the ships leave behind as they fly.

Not all of them are round, as there is also a long narrow model in the shape of a cigar, which can transport hundreds of people. Therefore, not all of them have the same shape and size. These are the transport vehicles of other planets.

The crews of these spaceships communicate with each other telepathically, without telephone, television or using anything like that. They have all their faculties awakened.

Any of those inhabitants of the Earth who brags very loudly, such as the North Americans and the other powers, who believe themselves to be the only ones with knowledge: what are those poor ignorant people doing without really knowing the wonders that exist on other planets?

The interplanetary spaceships of the extraterrestrials are ready and prepared to take off and to rescue all those people who work according to the formula that is given in this book. The extraterrestrials are informed, so it is not necessary to call them because they know us inside out. These ships will be the rescue when the moment arrives. There are very few who will succeed, they can be counted on the fingers of one hand. This is because nobody wants to work, but instead they take everything to the mind. From the mind come theories, as it is the same ego bringing them out, and what we need here are actions: to begin once and for all the work we have to do.

I give this report with the aim that everybody finds out the truth once and for all: we are not the only inhabitants of our solar system and our galaxy. Instead, we are the lowest ones. The countries that believe themselves to be great powers think that they know everything, but they are proving just the opposite with their actions. Through the atrocities they are carrying out against themselves and others, the quality of our Humanity is proven. I do not swallow those stories that they are inventing because I know for sure.

I am writing this book so that Humanity can see how the North Americans and scientists have taken them in with sheer lies and threats. What I am saying I will stand by always, and if I have to die to uphold the truth, so I will die.

THE DEATH

This chapter is given the esoteric title "The Death", because the one who begins to disintegrate his defects starts to leave the circle in which the whole of Humanity sits. So when he is asked to commit a misdeed, the others say: "He is not much use, he is a dead person", because he does not follow the rest of Humanity.

Every human being carries a Divine Spark within, called the Soul, Buddhata or Essence. Well, it has various names, but in reality it is a Divine Spark which gives us stimulus and strength to begin a spiritual work, such as this one I am teaching you here. This Essence or Soul is trapped in all of our wickedness, defects or psychological selves, which esoterically is referred to as the "Ego". They are the ones that do not allow the Essence to express itself freely, because they are the ones who take over the voice and control of a person.

But through the work of the disintegration of the defects, the Essence grows, becomes stronger, and manifests with more clarity and with more strength. It is gradually transformed into the Soul.

I will give you an example: this tree is supported by its main roots, they do not feed it, but only hold it up against the wind and its own weight,

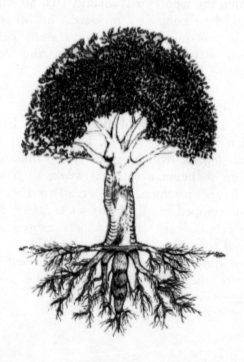

so that it does not fall down or collapse. And its tiny roots are the ones that spread along the surface of the soil and absorb sap to nourish it.

Such is our Ego or that of Humanity: the thick roots, which hold up the tree, symbolize the main defects like lust, revenge, anger, pride and many others. And the small roots represent the details: those tiny manifestations that belong to such and such a defect, which we do not see as a defect but in fact they nourish it. The Ego is fed by all these tiny small details, of which we have a large number.

We must begin to observe ourselves, to see the thousands and thousands of negative details that we have, and which sustain the trunk. Everybody who wants to be saved from the coming disaster needs to act in this way: to get down taking the nourishment away from this tree, by getting rid of the tiny small roots. Negative details like bad thoughts, hatred, envy we feel towards other people, ambition, taking coins and insignificant things, telling lies, saying words full of pride, greed; well, all these things which are basically negative; one must start to disintegrate them in a serious way.

There is another Divine Spark within us, called the 'Divine Mother'. Her task is to disintegrate the defects with a lance she has. However small the detail may be, you need to ask the inner DIVINE MOTHER: **"My Mother, pull this defect out of me and disintegrate it with your lance".** She will do so, because it is her task to help us in this way so that we can liberate ourselves. In this way the tree will stop growing. Instead, it will get undernourished and it will wilt.

What I am teaching here is to be put into practice, into action: wherever you go, whether you are working or whatever you are doing, you need to pay attention to the mind, the heart and the sex. These are the three centers where every defect manifests itself. When an element is manifesting, through whichever of these three centers it may be, the petition to the Divine Mother must follow immediately, so that she can disintegrate it.

Through this work of the death of the ego that I am explaining, we gain Scientific Chastity and we learn to love Humanity. Anyone who does not work upon the disintegration of the defects, can never reach Chastity and can never reach the point of feeling love for others, because he does not love himself.

The disintegration of the defects and the astral unfolding are the ONLY FORMULAS we have to be rescued.

ASTRAL UNFOLDING

Dear Reader:

As we speak about the astral, I want to ask you whether you have dreamed about people who passed away years ago, about places and people you do not know physically. This is what people normally call dreams: "Last night I dreamt such a thing". However, nobody stops to think about why they have dreamed about other regions or places, while the physical body was resting in bed.

This is the Astral Plane or Fifth Dimension, where neither weight nor distances exist, and to which the Astral Body belongs. This is a body exactly like the physical, energetic, which moves at great speed like a thought and is able to investigate everything we wish from the Universe.

In the Fifth Dimension we move, we explore and we know what the Angels, the Virgin and all the Hierarchies are; they move, speak and teach a Wisdom that is not written in books and is beyond the human mind. When someone want's to know on his own that which people call Occultism, over there one knows it and it stops being occult.

The important thing is not to leave unconsciously, asleep, but to consciously leave the physical body and move completely at will. My dearest reader, if you are going to put into practice the astral unfolding. I will give you mantras that I have used and I know that they give positive results. A mantra is a magic word that allows us to leave the physical body and to return to it, with full consciousness.

You lie down, relax your body and say the magic word three or five times verbally. Then you continue by repeating it mentally. When you feel that a current is running through your whole body from the feet to the head, as if you were losing strength, and you feel a lethargy so that you do not want to move. Then, you must rise with extreme care. Without disturbance, get up, do a little jump and at once you will float.

Do not be afraid, surprised or overjoyed when you see that you are floating in the astral body: all human beings do it and nothing has happened to them. It is only that they leave unconsciously and do not act at will.

We all have our Divine Spirit, called the Father. As soon as you see that you are floating in the air, say: "My Father, take me to the Gnostic Church," or to wherever you want to go or wish to know, and he will take you there immediately, as fast as lightning. There, you will receive the teachings directly from the Hierarchies.

In this way you are beginning to gain the true Wisdom, which is neither written in books nor taught in universities or anywhere. Hopefully you will do it every night

Mantra **LA RA S:** this mantra is pronounced so that the sound of each syllable is prolonged:

Lllllaaaaaaaaaaaaaaaaaaaaaaaaaaaaaa
Rrrrrrrrrrrraaaaaaaaaaaaaaaaaaa (rolling the r).
Ssssssssssssssssssss (like a hiss).

Another mantra for unfolding with the astral body
is: **FARAON**

Faaaaaaaaaaaaaaaaaaaaaaaa
Rrrrrrrrraaaaaaaaaaaaaaaaa
Ooooooooooonnnnnnnnnnnn (rolling the r)

I am going to give you another key to awaken
consciousness in the higher dimensions:

Everything we see here around us, houses,
people, cars, has a double, which is the astral.
If you want to discern where you are, whether
you are in the physical or in the astral, look at
everything that is around you, people, houses,
the place, and ask yourself the question: "Why
am I seeing this or that?" with wonder. "Am I in
the astral body or in the physical body?" And
you do a little jump with the intention of
floating.

It is not necessary for you to jump a meter:
with some centimeters that you raise yourself
from the ground you already know whether
you are there physically or not. If you do not
float it is because you are in the physical, but if
you float it is because you are in the astral body.
Then, when you notice that you are floating,

you need to ask the Inner Father immediately to take you to the Gnostic Church or to a place you would like to know about.

Do it daily, as often as you can do it during the day, while you are working or wherever you are and you will see the results.

I stand by what I have written in this book, because I know it. I am sure about what I say because I have investigated thoroughly with my astral body, which allows me to know about everything in great detail.

CONCLUDING REMARKS

I am giving these formulas to Humanity, because those who really want to be saved from the forthcoming catastrophe must start immediately to disintegrate the psychological self, that means all our defects, which number thousands. They need to be prepared, so that at the time of the rescue they are taken to a safe place, where nothing will happen to them and where they can continue working on themselves until they reach Liberation. That is the one who will manage to escape the disaster.

The Divine Justice describes this Humanity as "the lost harvest". That means there is nothing that can be done. The forthcoming destruction is happening because the Gods can do nothing more for us. Therefore, nobody will surprise the Hierarchies: everything is planned.

Dear reader: I am speaking very clearly so that you understand the necessity to start working seriously. Whoever is working will be rescued from the danger. This is not for you to make theories or discussions out of. Instead, the true teaching that I am giving in this book needs to be experienced. There is nothing else to which we can resort.

I am not a fear-monger, I am a human being warning of what will come and happen. This what I am saying to you here is very serious. Whoever fears God begins to work against the defects, which are separating us from the Father.

I could write more about the esoteric part. However, I do not want to take your time but fight so that each one carries out this work that I am teaching. This is the way to follow and I do not want anybody to get lost.

Dear Reader

If you re interested in some more information, you can contact:

C. Volkenborn Verlag
Postfach 11 16
63611 Bad Orb, Germany